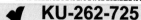

KU-262-725

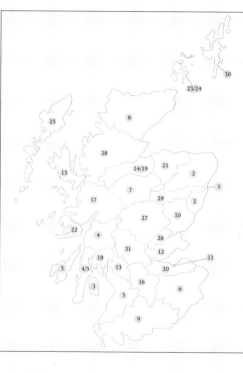

1. Aberdeen
2. Aberdeenshire
3. Arran & Ayrshire
4. Argyll
5. Southern Argyll
6. The Borders
7. The Cairngorms
8. Caithness & Sutherland
9. Dumfries and Galloway
10. Dundee & Angus
11. Edinburgh
12. Fife, Kinross & Clackmannan
13. Glasgow
14. Inverness
15. The Isle of Skye
16. Lanarkshire

17. Lochaber
18. Loch Lomond, Cowal & Bute
19. Loch Ness
20. The Lothians
21. Moray
22. Mull & Iona
23. Orkney
24. Orkney in Wartime
25. The Outer Hebrides
26. The City of Perth
27. Highland Perthshire
28. Ross & Cromarty
29. Royal Deeside
30. Shetland
31. Stirling & The Trossachs

The remaining four books, Caledonia, Distinguished Distilleries,
Scotland's Mountains and Scotland's Wildlife feature locations
throughout the country so are not included in the above list.

PICTURING SCOTLAND

CAITHNESS &
SUTHERLAND

COLIN NUTT
Author and photographer

2 In the midst of Sutherland's far-north wilderness: just after dawn on a winter's day, the two great bastions of Arkle (787m/2582ft) rise up on the far side of Loch Stack. Compare with pages 46 and 4[

CAITHNESS & SUTHERLAND

Welcome to Caithness & Sutherland!

Among the many worlds of Scotland, the northernmost part of the realm is indeed a place apart. A large proportion of the North Coast 500 route reveals many of the wonders of this region. This is not a journey to be hurried, as the landscape dictates the pace, for example where sea lochs extend, fjord-like, miles inland. While some are now bridged, others add miles to the journey. But before we get too carried away, it is important to remember that they were once two distinct counties which became joined politically due to the forming of a single parliamentary constituency from 1918 to 1997. Very different in character, Caithness is a wide-open world that embraces the peat-land 'Flow Country' on the one hand and fertile agricultural plains on the other, while Sutherland is a land of wilderness, extraordinarily shaped mountains and is one of the least-populated parts of Western Europe.

One thing that Sutherland and Caithness share is an abundance of water, stored in countless lochs and lochans, flowing through endless burns and rivers. The surrounding seas have created (and of course are continually modifying) a most dramatic coastline, producing legions of towering cliffs, sea stacks, caves and arches. This process has been accentuated by the land having risen since the last Ice Age. So, although Caithness is lower lying than Sutherland, it shares these coastal features, with much of its landscape coming to an abrupt halt, high above the sea. Mankind's influence is far more noticeable on the eastern seaboard, where a coastal strip

Sutherland winter evening: looking west across the northern end of Loch Shin to the Ben More Assynt massif, the highest point in the county with a summit of 998m/3274ft.

has allowed the development of farming, and where inlets and estuaries have provided natural harbours for the fishing fleets. Sadly, this is also an area where man's inhumanity to man has been practiced in the Clearances that swept people away in favour of more profitable commodities. Those who eked out an already marginal living through subsistence farming were evicted to the remote coastal margins where they were expected to adapt to even greater adversity. Many did not stop at the coast, but took shipping for yet more distant lands. Much evidence of this period remains, as we shall see.

The starting point of this book's journey is Dornoch, Sutherland's delightful county town. With a history that goes back a thousand years, it has been the religious and administrative centre of Sutherland for 800 years. In a way, Dornoch seems out of place: northern Scotland is not supposed (is it?) to offer a town of such cosy charm that might be more anticipated on, say, the Galloway coast at the other end of the country. But that is a big part of its appeal, the

6   Dornoch's drinking fountain, presented by Miss Georgina Anderson in 1892.

...urprise of this tucked-away haven just where one might not expect to find such a place.

From Dornoch, we travel clockwise around the region. Initially, this means heading north-west across Sutherland over to its western coast, then weaving hither and thither up to the far north. There we turn east and head into Caithness, home of the most northerly point on the Scottish mainland. The final leg is down the east coast with one or two explorations inland. This is the part of the journey that takes in several of the abundance of ancient ritual sites, some of which go right back to Neolithic times. The sheer range of scenery, wildlife and built landscape add up to a unique experience courtesy of a unique land. And, if that's not enough, this part of Scotland is quite often treated to one of nature's most extraordinary phenomena, the Aurora Borealis (see back cover).

Plenty to do in Dornoch: the signpost points to the beach, the witch's stone, the golf course and more.

8 Dornoch Square is a gracious and fitting centre for a Royal Burgh, the status it was granted in 1628. The run of buildings from left to centre of the picture includes Dornoch Jail, The Courthouse and

Dornoch Castle (which was never actually a castle), built as the Bishop's Palace in the 16th century. Today it is a hotel.

10 Dornoch High Street seen from the Cathedral churchyard. Part of Dornoch's charm is the survival of traditional, independent shops such as the chemist on the right. There's a bookshop too!

To quote from a local website, 'There are grander cathedrals than Dornoch, but few so immediately **11** captivate the human soul. The red sandstone building exudes life and love.'

12 Gilbert of Moravia, Bishop of Caithness, founded Dornoch Cathedral in 1224. It has had a turbulent history and required major restoration work from 1835 to 1837. This is the East Window.

In totally contrasting style, this beautiful glasswork is a detail from the window donated by the 13 widow of Stewart Anderson, a former organist of Dornoch Cathedral.

14 The Dornoch Court House served the town for over 160 years until its closure in 2013. Today it house a variety of local businesses and has been re-named the Carnegie Courthouse after Andrew Carnegie.

At Historylinks, Dornoch. Top: two of a series of models portraying the conflict between Sigurd and **15** Maelbrigte. Lower left: recreated workshop of Royal Dornoch Golf Club. Lower right: early Christianity.

16 Dornoch beach boasts both soft sand and rockier areas. It is so extensive that it can be seen from miles away on the south side of the Dornoch Firth.

Dornoch is a world-renowned golfing venue. The Royal Dornoch Golf Course, designed by Old Tom Morris from St Andrews, is synonymous with some of the most famous names in the game.

18 Moving on from Dornoch, this viewpoint is on the south side of the Dornoch Firth in Easter Ross, but provides a good place from which to set the scene for what lies ahead. The distant snow-covered

mountain (opposite page) is Ben Klibreck, 28 miles to the north. Above, the north-west view takes in the Dornoch Firth, with Ben More Assynt rising 30 miles beyond.

20 The village of Bonar Bridge is situated at the head of the Dornoch Firth and until recent times was the lowest bridging point. The shape of the bridge is matched by the shapes of the clouds.

Looking downstream, more reflections and some brilliant autumn colour. Back in the pre-bridge **21** days of 1809, an overloaded ferry capsized near here, with the loss of 99 lives.

22 Upstream from Bonar Bridge, a southwards autumn view along the Oykel river towards the Kyle of Sutherland, with Carbisdale Castle just visible in the distance.

A few miles north of Bonar Bridge the River Shin thunders over spectacular waterfalls in a deep gorge. **23**
Inset: a salmon leaping up the falls.

24 A misty autumn dawn in Strath Oykel. As the mixed farming that can be seen suggests, this is fertile land. Norse invaders discovered its potential and drove out the Gaels who were living here then.

The name 'Oykel' is derived from the Norse *Ekkjal*. Strath Oykel is the traditional boundary between Ross-shire (to the south) and Sutherland.

26 To the north again is the village of Lairg, seen in the distance in this view from Ord Hill. The stones in the foreground are remains of a Neolithic chambered tomb dating from about 3000BC.

The largest area of fresh water in Caithness & Sutherland is Loch Shin which stretches 17 miles **27** northwards from Lairg. This view shows the landscape and land use around the loch near Lairg.

28 The introduction referred to Sutherland's extraordinary mountains and Suilven (731m/2398ft), seen here in the process of creating a cloud, is probably the most dramatic of all.

You'd hardly know this was the same mountain: in contrast to the picture opposite from the south-east, **29** this is Suilven from the south-west. The snowier slope on the right is part of Canisp (846m/2775ft).

30 Suilven saves its most dramatic profile for those who climb it. Pictured from the summit, this is the view along Suilven's ferociously steep ridge to its middle and eastern summits.

Taken from near the top of Suilven's very steep ascent, this northerly panorama shows off typical **31** Sutherland terrain and gives a preview of Quinag, the mountain range on the skyline.

32 Our first sight of Ben More Assynt was back on p.5; now, from the head of Strath Oykel, its long ridge looms above intervening hills and early-morning mist that fills the foreground.

In contrast to the slightly coy glimpse of Ben More Assynt opposite, here it stands proud in winter **33** glory, with the village of Elphin in the foreground – all in all, a classic Sutherland scene.

34 A few miles further north at Inchnadamph, a wind-blown pine tree provides the perfect framing for Quinag, with its Spidean Coinich summit on the left and Sail Garbh summit to its right.

Inchnadamph is at the eastern end of Loch Assynt where, on its promontory (virtually an island), **35** also stands Ardvreck Castle, 15th-century seat of the MacLeods of Assynt.

36 The view back to the south from Ardvreck includes Conival, Ben More Assynt's secondary Munro (Scottish mountains above 914m/3000ft), seen here at the right-hand end of the snowy ridge.

A scene which characterises Loch Assynt, where remnants of the Caledonian pine forest cling to the **37** rocky shores. The rock face in the background ascends almost vertically . . .

38 . . . as it forms the lower part of Quinag's western elevation. Compared to the distant view on p.31, this close-up emphasises its challenging western slopes.

Pushing on further north provides the chance to see the northern aspect of Quinag, which looks 39
nothing like the previous views. These are the buttress ends of Sail Garbh and Sail Ghorm.

40 We saw the northern aspect from Suilven earlier; here is the south-westerly panorama that overlooks Inverpolly and into Wester Ross. Once again, the wilderness nature of these parts is impressive.

Towards the left lies Loch Sionascaig, above which rises the dark profile of Stac Pollaidh (612m/2007ft). **41**
This area also features in the Ross & Cromarty and Scotland's Mountains books in this series.

42 The road along Loch Assynt goes to Lochinver, Sutherland's largest west-coast settlement. Above: Lochinver from Suilven. Below: this still, evening view shows how the village is wrapped

round the loch. Being on the west coast it is, of course, ideally placed to catch lovely sunsets.
n the foreground is the mouth of the River Inver, which flows down from Loch Assynt.

44 Journeying north from Lochinver, Badcall Bay demonstrates a different shade of sunset and another face of the coast, where a pattern of islands and skerries adds interest and fires the imagination.

Sutherland is rich in wildlife, including a huge variety of seabirds and waders – such as a **45**
Black-throated Diver like this one. Handa Island Nature Reserve is not far from here.

46 Next we take a south-easterly detour to see the mountains around Loch Stack. Above is Meall Liath Coire Mhic Dhughaill (801m/2628ft) – the longest name of any mountain in the Highlands!

This area is home to several of Sutherland's most notable mountains. This scene unveils the **47** mountainscape east of Loch Stack, with Arkle on the right and the long ridge of Foinaven on the left.

48 The first kiss of sun highlights the ridge and Ganu Mor, summit of Foinaven. At 914m/2999ft, it is as close as a mountain can get to being a Munro without being one, but Foinaven is nonetheless

ted by many walkers and climbers as one of Scotland's great mountains. It has four tops connected **49**
y a long, curving ridge. This is part of the ridge a bit later on the same day as the picture opposite.

50 The north coast of Sutherland is reached at the village of Durness, location of the amazing Smoo Ca[
Above is the entrance to this huge limestone cavern, the most dramatic coastline cave in Britain.

inside, it is even more spectacular, with a large waterfall cascading through the roof. Visitors can take a boat ride into the illuminated depths of the cavern.

52 Heading east out of Durness, it's just a short distance to this idyllic beach at Sangobeg. The Clearances in this area were met with some resistance, requiring a degree of military support.

The lengthy sea inlet of Loch Eriboll used to have a ferry before the building of the road. The promontory of Ard Neakie, seen here, was its eastern terminus, where disused limekilns also remain. **53**

54 Brochs are among Scotland's most impressive Iron Age buildings. Dun Dornaigil is a well-preserved example near Ben Hope (the most northerly Munro), which can be seen on the right of the picture

On a day like this, the start point of the path up Ben Hope is a most perfect spot. If camping here in **55** summer, enjoy the waterfall-shower! The summit (927m/3041ft) can just be seen.

56 The road network peters out in the far north-west, meaning some of the best locations can only be reached on foot or by boat. Sandwood Bay is a prime example. Often described as the most

magnificent beach in the UK, this picture shows why. The fact that it requires a four-mile walk from Blairmore only adds to the enjoyment by adding a sense of achievement.

58 Looking north from Ben Hope, Loch Hope is the nearer stretch of water, while beyond is Loch Eriboll – Ard Neakie (page 53) can just be made out on the extreme left of the picture.

Plenty of handsome Highland Cattle are to be seen in this area. These are by the road that runs **59** north-south along Loch Hope on the way to Ben Hope and Dun Dornaigil.

60 East of Ben Hope and south of Tongue is Ben Loyal, another flight of improbable fancy in the mountain-building stakes! This is its north face, seen from the Kyle of Tongue Causeway.

During the ascent of Ben Loyal, the views soon begin to open up. Patches of sunlight illuminate the **61** village of Tongue and bring a greenish tint to the sea. The summit of Ben Loyal is named . . .

62 . . . An Caisteal (the Castle). Left: sizing up climbing the hard way! Right above: male Ptarmigan (with orange eye stripe) on Ben Loyal. Right below: the female of the species.

The reward for the climb: wilderness stretches away to the east. Ben Loyal is not a great height at **63** 764m/2506ft, but the variety and number of the individual tops means there is plenty to explore.

64 Left: Red Deer are abundant throughout the north of Scotland. Stags are always an impressive sight. Right: back on the north coast near Bettyhill, the Pictish 'Farr Stone' stands outside Strathnaver Museum

A storm approaches Farr Bay. In the 'storm' of the Clearances, many people from Strath Naver came **65** to Bettyhill, which can be seen in the distance. Ben Loyal is just visible on the skyline.

66 Rough weather can add to the excitement of Caithness and Sutherland as the rapidly changing patterns of light on a stormy day add drama to the wilderness, as here at Loch Badanloch.

And so to Caithness, where we arrive at Thurso, Scotland's most northerly town. The central focus of **67** the town is Sir John's Square, with St Peter's & St Andrew's Church beyond.

68 Dunnet Head is the most northerly point on the mainland of Scotland. The Lighthouse was designed by Robert Stevenson and built in 1831. The Orkney island of Hoy lies in the distance.

The spectacular 100m/330ft cliffs of Dunnet Head are seen here from near the Castle of Mey, a few **69** miles to the east. The harvest is in and those round hay bales make a pleasing foreground.

70 The Castle of Mey was bought by the Queen Mother in 1952 following the death of her husband, King George VI. Immaculately maintained, it is her lasting legacy to Caithness.

The Dining Room at the Castle of Mey. The Queen Mother used to sit at the near end of the table.
The whole of the interior is a wonderful period piece which reflects the era of her ownership.

72 Coastal erosion makes for much spectacular scenery, such as here at Duncansby Head to the east of John o'Groats where there are many rock stacks to behold. Inset: Puffins are a great favourite among

he seabird population of the area and can be seen from May to July. This one has a beak full of sand
els, their favoured diet.

74 The Walled Garden at the Castle of Mey is separated into sections by mixed hedges, both to work as windbreaks and to create surprises around each corner, such as the Shell Rose Garden seen here.

Canisbay Kirk is a short distance east of the Castle of Mey and is where the Queen Mother worshipped while staying there. The church contains a plaque to her memory.

76 John o'Groats has built a reputation for being at the extreme north-eastern corner of the UK mainland, 874 miles from Land's End. Inset: the John o'Groats – Orkney ferry.

Keiss Castle's remains stand stark and austere on the stretch of coast between John o'Groats and
Wick. It was built by the 5th Earl of Caithness in the late 16th or early 17th century.

78 A few miles north of Wick, the remains of 14th-century Castle Sinclair Girnigoe are a scheduled monument and it is the only castle in Scotland to be listed by the World Monuments Fund.

Wick was the administrative centre of Caithness for nearly 500 years and became wealthy during the 79
herring boom. This view looks upstream along the Wick River.

80 Wick Heritage Museum is an excellent and surprisingly large museum. Left: the light from Noss Head Lighthouse; right above: a past fishing era re-created; right below: late 19th/early 20th C. room detail

To the south of Wick, the Old Castle of Wick stands in a similar type of location to Castle Sinclair **81** Girnigoe (p.78) – each one highly defensible above rocky 'goes' or inlets.

82 Loch Watten and the village of the same name are a few miles inland from Wick. On the right evening, it is a perfect place for sunset pictures.

Even the most inconvenient harbours have been used by fishing boats, notably Whaligoe Haven **83** south of Wick, to which a fearsome flight of about 360 steps was constructed over 200 years ago.

84 Inland from Ulbster is Cairn o'Get, a burial tomb that has been a feature of the landscape for 5,000 years. It is surrounded by prehistoric remains spanning thousands of years of human activity.

Loch Watenen, also near Ulbster, typifies the landscape of much of inland Caithness, where a **85** patchwork of small lochs provides the ideal habitat for all manner of wetland wildlife.

86 A little further down the coast at Mid Clyth is the Hill O'Many Stanes. Around 200 small stones remain standing, laid out in 22 rows. Their purpose may have been that of a lunar observatory.

Lybster village started as a planned development in 1802, some years after harbour facilities were **87** established in the 1790s. By 1859 over 350 fishing boats were based here. Today it's a little quieter . . .

88 Situated on a minor road north of Lybster, at 69.5m/228ft long, the reconstructed Camster Long Cairn shows Neolithic architecture on a grand scale. It may have begun as two cairns, a round one

and a long one, or may have been built as we see it now. Either way, these tombs were originally built more than 5,000 years ago, placing them among the oldest stone monuments in Scotland.

90 Laidhay Croft Museum is housed in a two-hundred-year-old, rush-thatched Caithness longhouse north of Dunbeath, which shows how people lived and worked in the 18th and 19th centuries.

Visitors can explore all the rooms from the byre to the comfortable-looking parlour pictured here. **91**
This includes one or two 20th century touches such as an early 'wireless'.

92 Spectacular or precarious? The setting of Dunbeath Castle could be thought of as either! However, as it has stood for about 550 years, its location must be more stable than it looks.

From Dunbeath, we take an inland detour to Braemore where an active croft is in the foreground, **93** backed by an attractive scattering of Scots pines with the rocky but shapely Maiden Pap rising beyond.

94 Beyond the Maiden Pap stands Morven, the highest summit in Caithness at 706m/2316ft. A 10.5-mile walk from Braemore takes in both hills, requiring 7-8 hours.

A dark picture to represent dark times: Badbea is the haunting site of a long-abandoned settlement. **95** During the Clearances, people were uprooted from the fertile straths inland and forced to live here.

96 The plight of the cleared peoples is evocatively captured in this statue named 'The Emigrants' a few miles down the road in Helmsdale. They look in opposite directions – past and future.

Helmsdale is a pleasing town in a beautiful setting by the mouth of the river of the same name. Its story is told at Timespan Museum & Arts Centre, housed in the long building to the right of the bridge.

98 Left: a few miles on is Brora, home of Clynelish Distillery, nowadays a modern distillery. This is the old building, no longer producing whisky. Right: Brora's impressive, castellated War Memorial.

Carn Liath Broch can be found next to the A9 between Brora and Golspie. Even in its ruined state, **99** Carn Liath shows the ingenuity and architectural sophistication of Scotland's Iron Age farmers.

100 If there were a prize for the most 'fairytale' castle in Scotland, Dunrobin would be the winner. Although it goes back to the 13th century, what is seen today dates to the mid 1800s.

There is much French influence (e.g. the conical spires) blended in with the Scottish Baronial style.
The garden is based on those at the Palace of Versailles, but with the benefit of a sea view!

102 The railway here was privately built by the third Duke of Sutherland, opening in 1870 and running from Dunrobin to Helmsdale. Today's charming Arts & Crafts-style station dates back to 1902.

A small flock of Greylag geese fly over the photographer in east Sutherland. It was probably a short, **103** local flight, as they were flying quite low and not in the usual 'skein' formation.

104 Golspie is south of Dunrobin Castle and its history is bound up with that of the Earls and Dukes of Sutherland. It is a pleasant and well-maintained town, as this picture of Main Street shows.

It boasts many attractive buildings such as these charming cottages at the north end of the town. **105**
The 1834 statue to the 1st Duke of Sutherland can be seen on the distant hill top.

106 This is the bridge at the end of The Mound, a causeway across Loch Fleet, completed in 1816 to eliminate the last ferry crossing between London and John o'Groats. The apparatus on the bridge

...perates the sluice gates that control the flow of water beneath. The picture above is taken from he Mound, looking inland (westwards) up Strath Fleet with rowan trees in the foreground.

108 With the ruins of Skelbo Castle on the left, this is Loch Fleet looking towards The Mound. Loch Fleet is one of Scotland's National Nature Reserves, a rich habitat for wading birds and sand dune flora.

With much wildlife to see in addition to its obvious scenic charms, on days like this Loch Fleet is a **109** tranquil and relaxing place to spend some time.

110 Seals can often be seen basking on sandbanks or rocks, sometimes quite close to shore. These are taking it easy at low tide on Loch Fleet, a little to the north of Dornoch.

Our journey has come full circle, so let's finish on a high note by way of this aerial view of **111** Loch Fleet, which gives a unique perspective on this lovely tidal basin.

Published 2017 by Lyrical Scotland, an imprint of Lomond Books Ltd, Broxburn, EH52 5NF
www.lyricalscotland.com www.lomondbooks.com

Originated by Ness Publishing, 47 Academy Street, Elgin, Moray, IV30 1LR
(First edition 2013 published by Ness Publishing)

Printed in China

All photographs © Colin and Eithne Nutt except pp. 4, 45 & 73 © Laurie Campbell; p.64 (left) © Sue M. Cleave;
p.76 inset © Paul Turner; pp. 111 & back cover © Scotavia Images

Text © Colin Nutt
ISBN 978-1-78818-001-6

Front cover: Ardvreck Castle, Loch Assynt; p.1: Kylesku Bridge replaced a ferry from 1984; p.4: Puffin;
this page: at Pulteney Distillery, Wick; back cover: Northern Lights

While the Publisher endeavours to ensure the accuracy of information provided, no responsibility
can be taken for errors or omissions. The publisher welcomes information should any be found.